AFTERFEAST

PREVIOUS WINNERS OF
THE DORSET PRIZE FOR POETRY

Landon Godfrey *Inventory of Doubts*
Selected by Dana Levin

Jesse Lee Kercheval *America, that island off the coast of France*
Selected by Ilya Kaminsky

Mario Chard *Land of Fire*
Selected by Robert Pinsky

Thomas Centollela *Almost Human*
Selected by Edward Hirsch

Lauren Camp *One Hundred Hungers*
Selected by David Wohjan

Maggie Smith *The Well Speaks of Its Own Poison*
Selected by Kimiko Hahn

Jeffrey Harrison *Into Daylight*
Selected by Thomas Sleigh

Ruth Ellen Kocher *domina Un/Blued*
Selected by Lynn Emanuel

Rusty Morrison *After Urgency*
Selected by Jane Hirschfield

Joshua Corey *Severance Songs*
Selected by Ilya Kaminsky

G.C. Waldrep *Archicembolo*
Selected by C.D. Wright

Sandra Meek *Biogeography*
Selected by Jeffrey Levine

David McCombs *Dismal Rock*
Selected by Linda Gregerson

Amaud Jamaul Johnson *Red Summer*
Selected by Carl Phillips

Rachel Contreni Flynn *Ice, Mouth, Song*
Selected by Stephen Dunn

Ilya Kaminsky *Dancing in Odessa*
Selected by Eleanor Wilner

"These brilliant poems are covertly grounded in metaphysical questions, such as: Where is the line between one's ever-evolving consciousness and the only slightly more static 'material' world? And the brain, is that behavior or matter? And love, what's that? To explore these questions, vast categories and fluid distinctions are fractured and then woven back together to create an oracular, constructed self—a like-minded speaker, who, like us, has five senses as well as countless more that extend perception into other realms. This speaker lives in a dream world of her own making that is set, like a body inside its skin, in the real world that chance has granted her. She—American, Jewish, lesbian—lives inside history and dislocation, inside death and its sister, persistence ("rotgut of pine needles. / Bees do a deathhurdle over the edge, yet I do not transform"). In 'Kavala,' titled for the ancient Greek city that was once known as Neapolis (new city) the moon says: 'I // tell you / what this silence stands for'. The voice of the timeless lyric moon is the poet's voice. Her voice becomes the voice of Time talking to Space about what it is to be human. And yet, in the world of these poems, as in our world, we also have Formica, Pringles, melting butter and a matching yellow swimsuit. In other words, we have all the realities: the real, the surreal, the unreal, and the existential irreal. We need them all because any self, poetic construct or flesh-and-blood, inhabits all of these and stays busy trying to make sense of the ways in which they intersect."

—*from the Judge's Citation by Mary Jo Bang*

AFTERFEAST

Lisa Hiton

T|P

Tupelo Press
North Adams, Massachusetts

Library of Congress Control Number: 2021934629
ISBN-13: 978-1-946482-56-3

Cover art: Georgia Theologou, *How to disappear completely*; Oil, acrylic
on canvas. Oil on cotton/linen. 30 x 40 cm. Used by permission of the artist.

Cover and text design by Bill Kuch.

First paperback edition October 2021

Tupelo Press
P.O. Box 1767
North Adams, Massachusetts 01247
(413) 664-9611 / Fax: (413) 664-9711
editor@tupelopress.org / www.tupelopress.org

Tupelo Press is an award-winning independent literary press that publishes
fine fiction, non-fiction, and poetry in books that are a joy to hold as well as
read. Tupelo Press is a registered 501(c)(3) non-profit organization, and we
rely on public support to carry out our mission of publishing extraordinary
work that may be outside the realm of the large commercial publishers.
Financial donations are welcome and are tax deductible.

CONTENTS

PASTORAL

It doesn't have to be
something that happened to us
for me to write it. Finally
I have to arrive
in the field of what is
unsaid, and I am in it now, arrived there
as though it were a memory,
which is not the same as being in a body:
unreal in one sense, real in another—
when we were children, the autonomy of falling asleep
near each other
presented itself to me
as insidious, as squinting in dim light
to rack the focus and switch what is sharp:
I thought I wanted a sister.
What I wanted was a lover.

THEORY OF UNIVERSES

In another version we are eating eggs for breakfast.
In another version there's oatmeal on the stove. In another version
it's 1851 and we come in from a hunt to hang the rabbit over the fire.
It can't be the same but the light is
so you know it's still November.

In the one with the eggs we're sitting at the table and you say
Pass me the Life section.
With the oatmeal we're sitting at the table and you say Here.
You move to the back of my chair
and almost touch me but there's the bowl of brown sugar

again. I wake up in a room filled with file cabinets:
images in many folders. The images are cadavers.
They are cadavers. They are not of cadavers.

I tell myself I'm a librarian, but I'm not sure what to do
with all those bodies I don't want.
Tell me what the labels say. Do not
touch? Anniversary of ice?
The only body I want to study isn't in the mausoleum.
I wake up in a clearing. Tiny votive candles

lining the sycamore tree called "Incredible Monster."
Slabs of ice titled "5th Anniversary." The one body I want
to study isn't in the clearing, isn't back at the hotel room.
It's in the basement at a party
against the brick inlay. This time
you move to the bed with Conor. This time you go to the car
with Alex. In 1851 I try to shoot Russell
but I kill a rabbit instead. But I kill you instead. But I'm bleeding

out. The light is the same
and we are waiting for snow in all the tiny worlds.

MOON CHILD

I think of these things to tell you when you are asleep:
Little pools of water filled with limbs. The sky is dull,
The sky in excess. I draw rings around your belly.

Sometimes I do things to you because I want you to do them to me.

In the morning, when you are still asleep, I reach my hand
Into your mouth, down through your chest. I turn your heart over.

TUESDAY

You wear a yellow bathing suit
    You leave the butter   melting on the stove
                sizzling in the kitchen.

   We are standing

somewhere between
  door and sunlight.

         You take the burrs out of my skin.
         They're made of ice.

You say   are you alright?   I look at your hand:
            all the things that sting me
              in your palm
            then on the floor.

The little holes in my arm   still burn.

     Shh, shh...   you say   and touch my arm—

    your breasts
in the bathing suit   the butter
        burning in the pan.

VIGIL

Sweetly, tell it sweetly. When the inner tides stir me,
I spend the first minutes memorizing the lover,
her chest in waves, her cheeks, edgeless. The precipice

of the balcony from which my feet hang over
the clematis vines, these nocturnal devotions.
Coming toward me, a prologue, a flying orchestra

of spring birds gathering on the banks of the creek.
To what are they praying? To what do they give such praise?
The landscape will change soon, filled with gold

light. When the inner tides stir me, the first minutes
are turmoil, memorizing the lover, being inarched
to night. What the birds tell me, they tell sweetly:

I am the hull of a boat, washed up to an island shore,
looking sideways at what is vertical in the landscape:
the dawn breaking in the space between trees.

THE SPACE BETWEEN TREES

"the trees and the trees and the / space between the trees,
swimming in gold."

–Richard Siken

I.

Go into the garden and pick the tomatoes.

They're ripe as a dream. Imagine me naked

making a dinner. Goat cheese, arugula,

fresh strawberries staining Formica. Imagine being

threatened by something so awkward and timid. I am not

naked. I am not brave. The world is never mentioned.

When we are young, we are inside our narratives

climbing trees because we cannot fly. Picking apples

from our fathers' shoulders. Catching fireflies

in our hands. Open your hands now. Fireflies leaving you

gasping for air. We hold on to things because

we think proximity to the world makes us a part of it.

Call me from the garden. I want to make sense of it.

II.

Call me from the river. I want to make sense of it—

the clipped phrases, the muttering of words. There's a house

party going on in the background. I cut the lemons. I cut the lemons

off-center. Marrakech, pigweed in the gardens of Thasos,

the bartender, the book I gave you with the broken spine.

The word was never mentioned. Stand closer to me,

taste the sauce, I'm making it for you.

III.

For years the entomologist studies the species he loves,

only what if he's not an entomologist, what if he's you,

and what you find is too familiar so you cut it into pieces.

Farewell body, farewell village, farewell window with the amaranth

flourishing in the morning frost. I'll dig a tunnel for you

where we can live secretly away from the light.

If the tunnel floods during August storms, cicadas

will crawl up over us to die in the sun. I want to say

the word out loud, but I have no voice.

Where is the shovel? Where is the hammer?

IV.

We built a garden but we forgot to build ourselves

a cathedral. Light beams in as certain colors.

I want to make a mythology out of the image

in the window, you picking tomatoes.

It always rains on the lover before she dies.

Two figures moving to opposite sides of a map.

Look closer. The map is a garden. The figures begin

as pawns, are revived as queens.

Now, the moment when it's no one's move,

that's what the poem is, the space between trees,

the landscape of distance, which is a longing,

which is a hunger, which is what makes us

lines on a page reaching from one trunk to the other

but there is no telling between the two.

Only air, only light, only the absence of flesh.

V.

Your heart is so small and delicate. Your heart beams

like citrus. Here are the pores opening. Here are lovers

ripening in a purple sky, the space where there is nothing

between. Face me. Leap into it. The lines blur

like watery lenses. We are not mythology. Neither are we

love. There, I said it. Now close your eyes. Leave me

standing in the kitchen, water flooding in from the storm.

Wanting to be extraordinary we made ritual out of our tiny lives.

I'll tighten the screwtop on the bottle of balsamic.

I'll leave the knives in the drawer.

VI.

There is a myth about love and I read it over

and over. Every night you dispel it

by putting other bodies between us. How

does this end? Do I wash up on a shore covered in green

glass? It was supposed to be harmless, the smell of vanilla

and thyme in the crook of your neck where skin meets hair.

Your harpooned jaw. How we are afraid of the same thing.

VII.

It won't be your body I miss when I'm alone (gunmetal

winds against the French windows)—I left the mollusk shells

on the sill in the kitchen. In South Carolina, you gutted them

and listened inside. It was beautiful to you the way opera is

to your mother, a language you cannot translate

but that you feel more deeply than your own.

THE LYREBIRD

Tail plumes stretched like sharp swords, then recoiling. I followed it
        thinking it was
a kookaburra. With every inch I advanced, it changed

its song—unrecognizable cries, stolen from the throats of others. Liar.
Liar bird. Holding still, the feathers like byzantine paintings of snakes.
        Can't fly.

Foul in your originless body. You try to be everything and are therefore
nothing. It wasn't about the trees being felled

until you railed on as the chainsaw.
And like Orpheus with the lyre, you faced your doom and sang into it.

DREAM OF MY FATHER'S SHIVA, LAKE MICHIGAN, 1963

I pull a body out of the lake and it's my size.
You are completely dry.
I drag you across the beach by the right arm
and right leg. I bring you to the shiva house.
It's easy because you grip my hand.
I don't have to do all the work.
Your other hand is missing fingers.
I trawl you back to the lake to find them.
Your freckles enumerate
and cluster, constellations, little myths
I flick off your skin like sand.
The sand dissolves into snow, which turns
to ice. I slide with you,
ice skating children playing on a snow day.
Faces of the family around the shiva table
seasons later, years later, waiting for us
to return from this desert of ice.
The hours, they come as an urn
to put you in. You do not fit
anywhere else—the mind, the house, the vase...
I am not prepared for the change:
when the grip tightens and then slacks,
it's winter, it's summer.

KINZIE BRIDGE

When the stranger's fist
slams into my shoulder
I know that I've done something
wrong in this life.
He's listening
for a sound like cutting
through an eggplant: hollow, spongy.
He hits again, still no touch of my
marrow of a cow spread on toast points
four months ago in Boston.
A delicacy, the waiter told my aunt, tastes
like the offspring of butter and fat. And it did.
On the third hit, the gong rings
in me, only for me,
and I am Orpheus
turning, staring into his face,
his fists hoisted, boxer's stance,
he won't look into my eyes
and it's the instant I know
it's all wrong, this life,
it's something I've done.
I turn to banish
my violence:
you better hope you can run faster than me, fucker.
The arc between his knuckles
makes the bridge you run across:

at one end, your life;
at the other, a clearing.

VARIATION ON TESTIMONY

I turned before I got in the truck, and in the moment before
desertion I noticed his hair: dunegrass, the blond arcing, the only thing left
in motion. I get hard. I get gone—

the tires screech and I'm watching the dream in third person: pan out
on dust rising over God's country. *God's country.* Later, the body
will be shittied by birds. The fence without varnish
                                    digging into his spine.

LETHARGY

I am ill with history.
With watching it happen
and not belonging to it. In the efforts of
lesbianism, I have fallen
asleep. Light
through windows leaves your face
reflecting
what I'm sure I will die of
back at me, a magnifying glass
over the smooth hard body
in which I cannot exit. We act
like lovers, as if the manners of coming into existence
drop over us again and again like water,
and even though we are hard
bodies, the water, we know, means
never having foot to ground. I know this. The light
does not break through
the casing, yet I wait
for its violence.
I tell myself I want a lover.
          I want a lover.

THE SENATOR

I.

You go to The Senator's house
because it might be complicated

walking into the State House with your buddy's
nine caliber in your back pocket.

When he answers the door you try to talk
but he shouts

that he's not in the mood
to argue with someone who knows nothing

about politics. *Politics*, you grunt.
And then the gun comes out.

You aren't trembling. This surprises
you, but it surprises him more

because you seem to him
like his daughter—sweet

and blue-eyed
He's thinking:

isn't this the part where I press a button
and the wires pull me

up into the fly space
and the curtain closes?

But you know better, better than The Senator.
The curtain is already closed.

He asks you if you want
money. And you say:

Isn't this the part where you tell me
you'd rather have a dick in your face?

The gun is three inches from his nose,
pointing right between his eyes.

II.

The Senator stares down the barrel of your gun
but he doesn't see the gun at all:

summer, adolescence. He's in the back of his dad's car
with the first girl he's going to fuck.

He's distracted, only for a moment
by her hair

and how its tangles smell like ginger,
like his mother.

The girl thinks that she's going to kiss a boy
and then leave. He's surprised

when it hurts her. He's not scared
when he gets out of the car and she doesn't follow

because she's dead in the backseat.
It never dawns on him that you might shoot—

The Senator never thinks he will get shot;
only that he will get reelected.

He blinks, finally. And you drop the gun.
He has two choices now:

he can call the cops, or he can rough you up.
When he's got you against the brick of his house

III.

you know it's the part where you forgot to leave
yourself an out. Your eyes

are neither opened nor closed.
You know how this ends. (The gun

was fake, wasn't it?)
You are in the other place

now. You've been there once
before. It's not the same as numbness

where the scene is happening, but it looks all fuzzy.
It's more like being an insect:

everything is a deep dark
and you have to feel your way around.

IV.

This is the part where you tell him
you'd rather have the *gun* waving in your face.

You've said this once before,
only this time it's a dream. And in the dream

the gun is made of soap.
But in a murderous time,

(and this, comrade, is real now)

the stoop is not a stoop,
and The Senator is not a senator.

The brick wall is there
and your back is against it,

it pulls at the cotton of your summer self.
You were just inside. You were just

kissing. You were only eighteen.
No, it's that you're *already* eighteen.

You choose gun,
but it was just a game.

You don't get to choose.
There was no gun.

V.

Something is happening
with The Senator on the stoop

but you're still in the other place.
You get to dwell there a little longer

before the sun comes up.
Your blindness is not like The Senator's

because darkness is not the same
as blindness:

in the one case there's a curtain
keeping out the light.

The Senator stands in the doorway
knowing nothing of your murderous time,

how it passes, again, in beats: hands
thudding against your body.

Your father is roaming the streets somewhere
looking for someone to kill.

Sometimes when you're in the room backstage
you look for a door,

one that will open to a bright light.
Even in the theater of the mind

you know where everything is:
trap door to happy ending, trap door

to irreverence, trap door
after trap door, all the ways it might unfold.

But you remember: the sting of knuckles grazing brick
when you drag yourself from behind the building,

hailing the cab, you remember
the smell of clean hair.

KAVALA

I.

An old Greek man
with an arm raised

heiling
Pringle in hand

and the murder
of birds precisely

gingerly, taking
such communions

though I had left Berlin.

II.

The nonlovers
under the moon

having come
to a new country.

The moon
dusting its skin

a veil upon the Aegean.

III.

You'll want to open
your mouth

to hers, her mask
off, her arms

crossed.
I

tell you
what this silence stands for

says the moon
deep in your ear

so deep it's in your own
throat—

let the trees return
beneath me

so I may climb down
from my long hang;

there is no intimacy
in estrangement.

EPITHALAMIUM

It's the Aegean, windless,
rustling between blackness

and light. The boat
carries us to the rock shore. Rock

against wood, you cling
to me, ask me to drown

you out here.
Limbs are for trees, not bodies

I tell you. *Stay*
here with me. Stay.

The rocking of bodies
pressed together, all

red skin etchings.
This is not the last time we die.

Beneath the boat, waves take back
what they once offered: you,

your dress of skin hulling me
with its green luster

on your wedding day.
He, in the distance, beams

a green light:
If by water, I leave you.

AFTERFEAST

There is a deep-sea fish with two stones in its head. If you only find one stone, you've killed the fish too soon. You'll be doomed to seven years of bad sex. When you eat the fish, if you find both stones, run them under cold water with the lemons. At night, make a fire at the sea's edge. The stone you throw in the fire will kill the thing it represents. The stone you throw in the water is the thing you'll seek all your life. What the stones stand for has to do with the fish you ate. In one case, the stones stand for two horribly obvious things: love between women and Judaism. You can't know which stone is which. You can only know by the fate that comes after. Because you're a bad gambler, you won't sleep tonight. If you shatter them, it will be up to the wind. Throw both in the fire, you'll be a hollow corpse. Throw both in the water, you'll live forever like this. The day dawns, the bread rises, you were so beautiful, why couldn't you be brave?

HISTORIC STARE

Away from the ruins
we find a large town
with the same name
as the name of a man
you are forbidden to love.
Away from the ruins, more ruins.
You identify everything
by its rightful name—
the sewer : cloaca
empty space that convinces you of a civilization : agora
the marketplace, baskets of flowers, coins
passing through hands,
councilman gathering.
I cannot see
what moved in the grass
but I know it has a spine
and a heart. I
try to see
what is not there.
Soon, there will be others
milling near us.
I walk behind your shadow
never becoming it
though I ghost you,
your arms pointing,
pulled compass needles,
to where you know
we are going.

The sun is high now.

At the historic stair
you touch, I touch
soft silk stone.
I have to close my eyes
to imagine I'm in the agora.
You are in the agora.
Ahead of me you turn
(compass I cannot see
but I sense it
has a spine and a heart)
out from the sun,
from a silhouette
into yourself
and I am immersed in water
where there is no water.

THERE WAS AN ENTIRE CHICKEN

one from the spit where I watched them
spinning in the window while I waited for you
to go to the bathroom. A family with four young children
assessed the chickens,

skin throbbing over the burnt organs.
I thought the father was with his mistress
though I couldn't say why, nor could I decipher
the Greek volleying around

the chickens. The chickens
on my mind all the way to the coast.
Potos is crowded. On the beachwalk
there are many bodies.

There are no jobs. There is no money.
There are only beaches.
We walk along the smutty shops
lining the two streets of Potos.

The sun blares down.
I almost unbury it
on a hot day
in front of everyone.

I'd be the chicken on the spit.
I'd be long dead and burned.
I'd be daylight.

One cannot escape her sins
only survive them.

We arrive late to the table.
I don't know what Harry or Carolyn were thinking,
where they were before,
which of them ordered the chicken.

The chicken, as in love, is devoured.

GULLS, TOO

sense the fisherman
pulling the fish from the nets
over and over
this is how I mourned you
swimming to the cave, letting the birds
near me

LITANY

I gave away the sea.
It once moved me.

Here, when I raise my arms,
I leave no shadow.

I gave away the light.
So there would be

nothing
left to take from me.

I gave away
my hair, the silk

from my head, the blonder
threads from my limbs, from

the pubis—I'm all skin
now. If I keep

this up to bone
there will be no dark

left in me. I
gave away the parts—

the soul rose.
I had no hands to grasp it.

And so it got away
before I could give it.

The shore is a desert now.
I gave away the sea.

MISE EN ABYME

While the others clustered in
the inkwell of shade made by a beach umbrella,
we walked to the edge of the peninsula
just past the marble quarry.
The vast white slabs
burned in the midday heat,
burned at our feet. The crevices and indentations
that had just cradled tatters of waves
now dried and densely filled with salt,
ancient salt, scouring our callouses.
At the edge, I immersed myself
in the blue. Because the sky was
cloudless, I couldn't be sure
which element drenched my skin,
unbearable organ. The water,
then the slab. Immersion, then pain,
immersion, pain—and what had I desired?
and what had I seen?
No stone in my periphery,
no ships in the timeless clarity before me,
the blue spilling into itself and back,
and a voice speaking—
it began as hers
calling out to Alexander,
to his treasure
in the centuries-hollowed
drumlin below us—
then it morphed and hid in the shade
the same shape and color
as the shade of the umbrella,
made by the creature shaped like an umbrella,
its hood, hollow—is that the head
or heart of the thing?—and therefore
made of shade, structured to cradle
that dark mystery—voice

35

blotting itself until
it dissolved as everything else
into the invisible
crease of blue
only to return to me
as myself without a body—
immersion, then pain.
On the hot slab of history
I survived
and the creature below me
collected its things
in the shade of it.

THE HOUSES OF FRANKFURT

A stranger walks his dog toward the university.
It used to be a chemical plant.
There is a break in the plaza where students lie in the sun.
There is a tree taller than the buildings with a wide base.
The bark is black and the leaves are black as though it were a painting.
The shade is barely discernible.
The shade is barely discernible from the subject until I step into it.
It knows too much, the brightness.
Not every animal can survive it.
When I think of that city, first the tree.
Still abandoned houses.
Then the houses.
Too quiet for children. For dogs.
I look like no one in this city.

DREAM OF MY FATHER'S SHIVA, AUSCHWITZ, 1942

no water

as far as I
can see to the edge
of the relentless
field

a plow
homes

I hear
the violent
fanning

of a windmill
I am

at the steer
shoveling
bodies
to find you

when I think
gusts of it
there is something
humming

in the air of this
thick dream

cutting
through the pink smoke
I almost hear
you say it—

this lake of bodies
starts to freeze

I hear
your grunting
when the plow's hand
snags off your fingers—

Smokestacks
finally

in another world
it might mean
the city

where you taught me
about buildings

you're blue as Lake Michigan
when I get you in the machine's hand
the plow

turns to the building
with the lone smokestack

against my desire

ANCESTRY

Night will not fall for hours.
The air in the medieval town
is a gown of alwaysdark, dismissal,
                    and death.

        The pages of the book are blank,
then the pen in my hand
puts down the names. A lightning storm:

            LISA HARRI

            ALIZAH TSVI

            LOLITA MARCADO

Where we are, the mikvah rises.
You stop me from touching the water
saying the word *verboten*,
which swerves

                from that other century
through your cupped hand—
the song left out of the book, as in
your name:

        Night will not fall for hours.
        The Rhine is flooding
        ½ a mile down the road.

Where we are, the mikvah rises.

        Take me to the bakeries of your ancestors.
        Show me not where I would hide,
        But where they hid themselves.

43

BAKERY

Johannesstraße 1939

Spring rains bring with them humidity.
The blond, deepening. The curls,
irrefutable. Once,

I spent an afternoon alone
in your bakery. A young man stopped
outside,

watched me throw the flour.

We have been, always, a swivel.
A couple

revolving in opposed directions.

So many times, the young men who return
take you to the cellar
to indulge your mutual pleasures.

When this young man returned for me
you first were jealous,
then righteous

saving the bakery
saving me from the other Gestapo

by handing him the rolling pin—
which you first rubbed
with flour—

then the cellar key.

SODOMITE

what is fastened by
        the lover to the body
     then fortified by

        having been fastened to
    be copious, be deep
and can this have been

between only men
        or could they be women
     or have been feminine

imagine the world to be
        this too: copious, deep
     water, just like a great lie

still on the top when riling
        beneath, and heaving
     at the tide change when

below the surface static,
        mundane, non-love,
     unmoving murk of post-rain

we had once been yoked:
        exacting, platonic
     never ending

in action, though below
        us, copious
     amounts of igneous rock

fortified, so one could walk
       through the water
    in whatsoever form

it may take, intrusive body
      that pluton-
    lined orb divined

for even the righteous
       whosoever, by what term,
    fasten themselves

to anyone else
      by design

DISLOCATED CITIES

In the synagogue ruins, we stand
on opposite sides of a rock window
natural as 11th century figures
still acquainted with each other
as though no history had happened
through the rock lung.
You do not hear my sigh, exhale
when you inhale and think
Yes, Miriam.
My skin matted out by
the sun, dusty pearl, matching the ruins
we look through to each other.

*

A sign says *verboten*.
Because it is the language of your ancestors
you obey. This
is not the language of my ancestors
though there are Jews
who came from here.

*

We have never been lovers.

*

After the biergarten, after the river
drowning itself in the river,
after the long stroll through

the Rhinealley, music
in the vast cathedral
air from the crypt below
rising, centuries old
like the groundwater
below the synagogue ruins
just across the plaza. Judengasse
abandoned. The cathedral
where we are among a listening crowd. Pain
on the edges of my body
though bodies do not have edges
but are abstract and rounded.
The helix of music
is the helix of genetics
exhausting me, but waking you up.
It is so cold here.
I cannot cry for how numb I am
down to the breast.
We will never be lovers.

                    *

On the stone path leading to our pension,
a gravestone. Hebrew carved in
by German peasants.
They mimicked the shapes
but could not read
the names being written.
Another stone
left unturned / I cannot turn over. Another story
where the protagonist disappears
without a sound.

Twin beds in our room
bumped next to each other. I am cold
and sleep right away.

In the morning, you are awake
pacing. The news in German, the Rhine
still spilling into itself.
Where everywhere else I dream,
here nothing.
For breakfast: coffee, sausages,
a soft-boiled egg.
We'll find the bakeries
your family ran
before there was a war
to feel close to.

        *

You walk ahead of me
into the grand cathedral.
With my kino-eye, I recognize everyone
looks like you: medieval
and contemporary at once.

We stop for tea on the boulevard
leading up to the imperial clock.
Across the way, three street musicians.
Clarinet, accordion, tambourine,
the tune I know from the Hebrew,
at once medieval and contemporary,
at once a peasantry
next to the croon of the regal country. It was
the summer of Wagner
in the country of your ancestors.

        *

You stand before the buildings
that were once run by your family.
You ask me to take your photograph.

When I shoot through the glass
column, the lens flare, the light
so bright I see
black and white
like the photos you've brought
from the century before
which you folded and put in your notebook
boyish thing that you are:

If we are far, the war is far.

If I am close to you,
I am close to the war.

*

I am in the one country
where I have no affairs, where I do not feel
love. When I had no love
I excused anxiety
from the table and sent her
to her room in the attic
where she made no ruckus,
but when I slept alone
in the city of medieval air
I could hear
beneath the ice sheets
the low murmur of her
slow typing:

You can't get to Salonika
without passing through.

*

In the last city Reuben lived in
in Europe, I feel present
instead of historic. People
look like him, like my mother,
olive skin and coarse hair.
I ask where the right stones are.
I look for plaques to read.
I pace in and out of the hours.
The plaza where they burned the bodies
like banned books. The museum
tucked in the maze of Salonika.
Hide my face when I weep
sitting on the marble bench:
You would hide
me, you would hide me,
you would hide me,
if we were in a different time.
No one in my family
survived the Holocaust.
/
Everyone in my family
survived the Holocaust
though none is a Holocaust survivor.
/
Where were you
when the winds changed,
when you knew he would never be
Greek or Turk
because he was something else
without a nationality
but with a race
threaded thin as fishing line
all over Europe and heading west.
Was it in the shvitz house
next to a Greek Orthodox church.

Was it in a letter from the state,
a glance from his blacksmith,
a season of lemons that stayed green,
a lightning storm on the coast
of the city where so many bolts hit
at once, I had to believe in Poseidon.
Was this town Greek or Turkish
when he left. Was he a Turkish boy.
Were there poplars to swing from in the yard?

Greco-Turkish-Judeo-Spanish.
Yiddish. Hebrew. English. Hide

below deck, barrels of olive oil,
until you get to port.
Hide your face. Speak in Greek.
When they offer ouzo, ask for one
ice cube. When they offer yogurt
in the morning and they've already brought
ham and bread, say *efkaristo.*

                    *

You can't leave Salonika
without passing through.

You can't go back

        [to America]

without passing

        [through]

HISTORIC STAIR

Now that time has closed
its haggard mouth

I count my lovers in my head.
The broad stairs

to the agora are uneven, faded smooth.
I put my hands on every curve,

consider the masses, the feat
of turning stone to soft silk.

The ancient sewer fills
with the rotgut of pine needles.

Bees do a deathhurdle over the edge,
yet I do not transform:

I wandered the marketplace
purple-tipped lettuces, lemons, olive oil…

I had been trying to reach you.
I hadn't meant to do this to you

or myself. You were in another country
while I was in the ruins

and as in desire, I felt brave
but without rhetoric

until the sewer swallowed
and the bees became Virgil's

like you, drowned
in there, drowning, as I turn

away, and my failure lifts
and the word soars

out of that vast throat:
AGORA, followed by the bees

spit up as coins. Now
I sense that I'm the prisoner

as the figure staring into the narrow
body of me is not you, but is placing me

sideways on the stair. Now
there are many hands and feet

trampling through the agora. Now
when I tell myself I'm in the agora

the fears gather like eyes.

MAHLER'S NINTH

Gone, the pile
of shut black
mouths bowled
in cold

water. Gone
the thyme and tang of shallot,
as the garlic
burns in the oil.

They whir when strained:
shhh, let them think
we're already

gone. Does a thing remember
its ocean? Brine
like ragged
cement. Oh,

what thrill their lives were,
before the ice bath!
before the plastic bag!
In goes the white

wine and the fog
that rises from them
makes them drowsy—

why did I bring
something alive
into this kitchen,

in the wake of what struggle
am I to offer or perform
myself,

what was happening
in there, in those
blooming mouths—

so I peeked inside
through the steam,
obsessed with death
but having no desire to die.

TERRA VITA

My mother kneeling
next to the hibiscus
with a little hand shovel
planting hyacinths
when I came to watch her.

I must have been seven or eight,
wide-eyed at the vague thing
flopping in her hand.
She reached in, fumbled
through the soil. When she found

the other half of the worm
she placed it at the base of a flower
to show me that it was still alive,
that both halves were working
on their own, wriggling

back to their underground world
to be useful:

It's gorgeous in Boston today,
everyone is outside sunbathing
just like that day with the worm

and I know I had a dream about you
again. Or maybe it was your dream
and I was conjured to dwell there

so you wouldn't be alone. Why
I anticipate forgetting the clouds
today, their shapes, how lifelike

they are when they drift…why
I remember the worm…
it has something to do with skin

and pink smokestacks. My palms
red before callusing
after working at a steer,
or dragging a heavy load…

Oh God, you hath given me two hands
but only one heart.

IN RESPONSE TO TREES

In winter I knew them all
as one dead thing,

but now I love to watch them blossom.

The shortest tree
seems Japanese, translates

beauty into sunlike white and pink.

I lie under them
deciphering

their shapes. How to give a name
to something you know so well: Mother,

I know you are afraid

of my love
when I watch the little round discs fall

suicidally toward me. I am afraid

of what I might call them
while they are in the air…

                    Mother, I want to call them,
my Katarina, my riad, my morning floor,

tiny petals like eyelids
dropping down. The first time I dreamt

of falling
it was peaceful like this:—

nameless world, filled with green light...

      by what name, Japanese tree,
by what name, Mother?

HORSESHOE

Lately, I've been walking through arches.
Churches, synagogues, ashrams, no matter. I
find astonishment in the impulse.
The thought of my mother enters me in the monastery
even though I am Jewish
and I know I have not been good,
not heard her voice enough—she is still alive
but won't be always. Though this agony is
always. I do not find her
or anyone else I love in these buildings. But then,
what is it to love someone
if not to love the self,
which I have not, despite my banal fortune.
It was a profoundly depressing thought·
this afternoon in Cambridge, with the light holding
over the university, the steeples, the trees—and now
the thought is something else, is knowledge
in the way that it is known all at once
away from the guts
up in the mindfield: it's a running horse
beating your timid soul
knocking all over it with its metal-lined hooves
reminding you you are there.

THE BORDER

At night I watch you walk to the grotto.

What is said by the grotto
that you have not heard from me?
What failure sorrow is

when it departs with the sea.
I listen for the wind

to become dark, for the water's return.
But that is not the voice
speaking to you,

the waves finding your feet:
you're unknown and young,
you've never been pregnant,
the sound you hear

is not the grotto itself.
It is vowless, promising
nothing. Yet every night

I watch you walk to it
below the grove,
the olives reeking
in the late heat.

THE DWELLING PLACE
(OR, SCORING THE DEATH OF THE FIRSTBORN)

Έτσι, με την αναμονή, οι νύχτες μας έχουν επιμηκυνθεί
Μέχρι το τραγούδι έχει ριζώσει και να αναπτυχθεί σαν ένα δέντρο.
Και εκείνοι στη φυλακή, ω μητέρα, και αυτές μακριά στην εξορία
Θα αφήσουμε έναν στεναγμό και λεύκες ελατήρια σε φύλλα.

Did you notice the thyme blooming.
We'll walk again with a dooming in our feet,
The thunder thunder of sole on stone,
Until our bones carry us back again to the sea. O

We will not call it the sea! I have seen the night of the full moon
      Lighting the surface
      Of an intimate body.

Our bones will carry us to the sea and O! we'll say, O!
Let us reach below our feet and gather the stones, the wants
We vault into the air.

The stones that are round and smooth,
The stones that mean nothing, as bones mean nothing,
Except when offered to the well
Where tonight we have been exiled
Darling, let us run there,
Fledglings that we are,

Let us curse and curse and curse

At the thyme bursting open all over the streets,
For the chickens, for the tea,
For roasts and hosts of honeybees.

Do you trust this song as a gift upon a bough?
You must sing aloud what you feel is so:
I've lied to the Nazis. I've lied to the police. I've crossed myself

And crossed the streets. I sang Hallelujah! I sang it into the dark
Night, which opened its gate—Darling, Darling, it said,
I give you a new fate. Thyme

All over the landscape, thyme by the fields, thyme by the roads,
Olives and olives, toads and toads. The crickets
Have bandsaws for legs, yet cut nothing down,
But you, said the Night, can be a man about town.

> Gather the sprigs.
> Gather them like hearts.
> Sell them in the market.
> Sell them for their parts.

They call me the Knife! Lover like a young tree!
And in prison they made me an amputee,
A Boylston Street runner from that vast country.

Darling, they're replacing limbs with dollar bills,
They're checking us in to asylums they call hotels.
Sometimes the rooms play Wagner on a loop

In 4/4 time, the clef blurring, the chef
Who forgets the rind and the bodies of dead fascists.

So boil the water! Rub the meat with salt!
Stalin is dead and it's all our fault!
Shove an apple in his mouth when we get him off the spit,
Five sprigs for each limb will do the trick.

I was the firstborn. I saw
The streets before they were streets. I knew darkness as itself.
It was like being rigged to a ship
In mourning robes.

On the Bowery, young people flit in and out of clubs.

They lick each other and dream.
They do not ask questions.

Do they ask for the time?
Do they know how it grows? How it smells and feels and means nothing
Until you put it on the stove with the sourdough.

I didn't ask for this body. Darling, you have not been intimate
Or honest. The concrete below us
And the concrete above us are silent and rough.
The metal like the ship's bluff.

Who will mourn these dreams? The one about the moon
Where time stands still in the face of gravity.
Where chicken in the wood oven falls clean off the bone.
Where the young who gyrate are made of flesh
That has never been violated.

And who will massage the herbs into the meat.
And who will throw the stones in the well. I want to return
As a phoenix, but Jews don't get cremated.
How can I rise from this sleep, a heap
Of bones in a coffin,

If there is a tombstone, will you visit often?

After a while, you will ask for the time,
In the grocery store, in the car,
In the door left ajar

By the child
Who did not want to be naked, no. But Oh!
I have just been in the sea, which is to say born,
This is not skin for you to scorn.

You will ask you what happened in the name of the ghosts.
My grandmother has been in prison for ten years
And exile before that.

The screeching bats in summer fly low.
It is time to go. It is time to go.

Notes

"Variation on Testimony" takes on the grotesque and amoral "gay panic defense" posed in court after Matthew Shepard's murder on October 6, 1998 in Laramie, Wyoming.

"The Senator" used to be titled "Redefining Rape" after a 2010 bill was brought to the House floor that would have restricted both the definition of rape and a woman's ability to seek an abortion.

"Afterfeast" takes its title from the Greek. This great feast is attached to the Greek Pentecost. The Greek Orthodox church abides by the lunar calendar, which means that the Pentecost is, in fact, Shavuot—the Feast of Weeks. Shavuot marks the end of the seven week period between the Israelites being freed from Egypt and their being given the Torah. The week of Shavuot is marked by olives, dates, pomegranates, cheese, music, and parades. It is also a time in which those who practice must stay up all night to read and study the Torah.

"Historic Stare" is for Lauren Clark.

"Dislocated Cities" is for Richie Hofmann. And Carolyn Forché. And my mother.

The epigraph of "The Dwelling Place (or, Scoring the Death of the First-born)" is from *Eighteen Songs of the Bitter Homeland* by Yannis Ritsos. In "The Long Wait" he writes:

> So, in the waiting, our nights have lengthened
> Until the song has taken root, like a tree.
> And those in prison, oh mother, and those far away in exile
> They let out a sigh and a poplar springs into leaf.

Acknowledgements

Grateful acknowledgement is made to the editors of the following journals in which the following poems, sometimes in alternate versions, first appeared:

Anti-: "Afterfeast" and "Theory of Universes"
The Adroit Journal: "Variation on Testimony" and "In Response to Trees"
Cellpoems: "Gulls, Too"
The Common: "Sodomite"
The Cortland Review: "Mise en Abyme"
Cosmonauts Avenue: "Mahler's Ninth" and "The Space between Trees"
Denver Quarterly: "Ancestry"
DMQ Review: "The Senator"
Figure 1: "Dislocated Cities"
Foundry: "The Houses of Frankfurt"
Indiana Review: "Tuesday"
Hayden's Ferry Review: "Picnic"
The Journal: "Moon Child"
Lambda Literary: "Lethargy"
Leveler: "Dream of My Father's Shiva, Auschwitz, 1942"
Linebreak: "Epithalamium"
Nashville Review: "Litany"
New South: "Historic Stair"
PANK Magazine: "Kinzie Bridge"
The Paris-American: "The Lyrebird"
Poets on Growth: "Horseshoe"
Prodigal Magazine: "Pastoral"
The Shallow Ends: "Historic Stare"
Thrush Poetry Journal: *"Vigil"*
Tinderbox Poetry Journal: "Terra Vita"
Tupelo Quarterly: "The Dwelling Place
   (or, Scoring the Death of the Firstborn)"
Word Riot: "Dream of My Father's Shiva, Lake Michigan, 1963"
236 Magazine, Boston University's journal of alumni work, reprinted
   "Afterfeast," "Moon Child," "Lethargy," "Terra Vita," and "Tuesday."

Poets on Growth: An Anthology of Poetry and Craft reprinted "Epithalamium," "Litany," and "In Response to Trees," along with "Horseshoe."

"Dislocated Cities" and other poems won the AWP Kurt Brown Prize, selected by Tarfia Faizullah.

These poems would not be complete without the generosity of the following institutions: Boston University's MFA in Poetry, the New York State Summer Writers Institute, the Writing Workshops in Greece: Thessaloniki and Thassos, and 24 Pearl Street at the Fine Arts Work Center.

Thanks

To my readers, Richie Hofmann, Maggie Dietz, and Dan Kraines for your candor.

To TJ McLemore, Calvin Olsen, Sophie Grimes, and Megan Fernandes for your unrelenting support.

To Lauren Clark, who attended the Afterfeast. To Carolyn and Harry for sharing the table with us.

To my teachers, Maggie Dietz, David Ferry, Carolyn Forché, Louise Glück, Jorie Graham, and Robert Pinsky for the lineage.

To Jeff Berger-White for the books, for the poems, for the depths. For the hours.

To my parents—who have loved and supported the artist, together and apart.